Rooms Are Never Finished

Also by Agha Shahid Ali

POETRY

The Country Without a Post Office
The Belovéd Witness: Selected Poems
A Nostalgist's Map of America
A Walk Through the Yellow Pages
The Half-Inch Himalayas
In Memory of Begum Akhtar & Other Poems
Bone-Sculpture

TRANSLATION

The Rebel's Silhouette:Selected Poems (Faiz Ahmed Faiz)

OTHER

T. S. Eliot as Editor
Ravishing DisUnities: Real Ghazals in English (Editor)

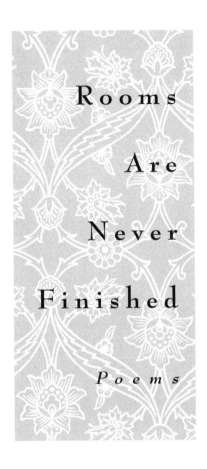

Rooms Are Never Finished

Poems

Agha Shahid Ali

W. W. Norton & Company
New York   London

For information about permission to reproduce selections
from this book, write to Permissions, W. W. Norton & Company, Inc.,
500 Fifth Avenue, New York, NY 10110.

The text of this book is composed in Weiss
with the display set in Bernhard Modern Bold
Composition by Molly Heron
Manufacturing by The Haddon Craftsmen, Inc.
Book design by JAM Design
Production manager: Julia Druskin

Library of Congress Cataloging-in-Publication Data

Agha Shahid Ali, date.
Rooms are never finished : poems / Agha Shahid Ali
p. cm.
ISBN 0-393-04149-2
1. Jammu and Kashmir (India)—Poetry. I. Title.

PR9499.3.A39 R66 2001
821'.914—dc21
2001034555

W. W. Norton & Company, Inc.
500 Fifth Avenue, New York, N.Y. 10110
www.wwnorton.com

W. W. Norton & Company Ltd.
Castle House, 75/76 Wells Street, London W1T 3QT

1 2 3 4 5 6 7 8 9 0

for my father—ASHRAF—

& for PARU, LALA & TUPALS

Contents

Acknowledgments

These poems—at times in different form—appeared in the following places:

The Agni Review "Hell," Part 3 of "A Secular Comedy," as "A History of Hell"
Ariel "Zainab's Lament in Damascus," "The Fourth Day"
Boston Review "Ghazal" ("I'll do what I must . . .")
Colorado Review "Heaven," Part 1 of "A Secular Comedy," as "A History of Heaven"
Grand Street "Eleven Stars Over Andalusia"
Gulf Coast "Barcelona Airport," "On Hearing a Lover Not Seen for Twenty Years Has Attempted Suicide"
jubilat "Karbala: A History of the 'House of Sorrow' "
The Kenyon Review "Summers of Translation"
The Massachusetts Review "Srinagar Airport"
Modern Poetry in Translation "The Nature of Temporal Order"
NEST: A Magazine of Interiors "Rooms Are Never Finished"
New England Review "God" as "There Is No God but," "Ghalib's Ghazal" as "Stanzas Shaped by a Ghalib Ghazal"
The Ontario Review "Above the Cities," "New Delhi Airport"
The Paris Review "The Purse-Seiner *Atlantis*"
Persimmon "Ghazal" ("I'll do what I must . . .")
Southwest Review "By the Waters of the Sind"
Tin House "I Dream I Am at the Ghat of the Only World," "Lenox Hill," "Memory"
TriQuarterly "Ghazal" ("In Jerusalem a dead phone's . . ."); "Earth," Part 2 of "A Secular Comedy," as "From Where I Knelt"
Washington Square "Rooms Are Never Finished" as "No Room Is Ever Finished"
Yale Review "Ghazal" ("What will suffice for . . .")

"Lenox Hill" was issued as a privately published broadside by Walter Feldman. It also appeared in *American Diaspora: Poetry of Exile* edited by Ryan G. Van Cleave and Virgil Suarez and, along with "Rooms Are

Never Finished," in *The New Bread Loaf Anthology of Contemporary American Poetry* edited by Michael Collier and Stanley Plumly. My immense gratitude (for reasons they may or may not know) to: Anjum Ahmed, Peter Balakian, Pengyew Chin, Michael Collier, Neil Davenport, Forrest Gander, Sara Suleri Goodyear, Daniel Hall, Ghulam Ahmad Lone (Ghulama) of Tral, Irfan Hassan, Muzamil Jaleel, Rafiq Kathwari, Anthony Lacavaro, Ghulam Mohommed Rather (Mahamdu) of Asham, Jeanne McCulloch, Christopher Merrill, Padmini Mongia, Anuradha Needham, Patricia O'Neill, Elise Paschen, Pavan Sahgal, Grace Schulman, Carol Houck Smith, Ellen Bryant Voigt, Chuck Wachtel, William Wadsworth & Vidur Wazir.

I pray you, oh, I pray: Don't die.

I'm here, alone, with you, in a future April . . .

—"Prayer to my Mother"

PIER PAOLO PASOLINI

On the shore where Time casts up its stray

wreckage, we gather corks and broken planks,

whence much indeed may be argued and more

guessed; but what the great ship was that

has gone down into the deep that we shall

never see.

—ANONYMOUS

To a home at war, my father, siblings, and I brought my mother's body for burial. It was the only thing to do, for she had longed for home throughout her illness. In 1990, Kashmir—the cause of hostility between India and Pakistan since their creation in 1947—erupted into a full scale uprising for self-determination. The resulting devastation—large-scale atrocities and the death, by some accounts, of 70,000 people—has led to despair and rage, then only rage, then only despair. Because both countries are nuclear powers now, international anxiety has increased: Kashmir, it is feared, may be the flashpoint of a nuclear war. The ongoing catastrophe—the focus of *The Country Without a Post Office*, my previous volume of poems—provides the backdrop to this volume. In January 1996 my mother came to the States for treatment of brain cancer. Till her death—in a hospital in Northampton, Massachusetts, on 27 April 1997—we were with her at my brother's home in Amherst.

Lenox Hill

*(In Lenox Hill Hospital, after surgery, my
mother said the sirens sounded like the
elephants of Mihiragula when his men drove
them off cliffs in the Pir Panjal Range.)*

The Hun so loved the cry, one falling elephant's,
he wished to hear it again. At dawn, my mother
heard, in her hospital-dream of elephants,
sirens wail through Manhattan like elephants
forced off Pir Panjal's rock cliffs in Kashmir:
the soldiers, so ruled, had rushed the elephant,
The greatest of all footprints is the elephant's,
said the Buddha. But not lifted from the universe,
those prints vanished forever into the universe,
though nomads still break news of those elephants
as if it were just yesterday the air spread the dye
("War's annals will fade into night / Ere their story die"),

the punishing khaki whereby the world sees us die
out, mourning you, O massacred elephants!
Months later, in Amherst, she dreamt: She was, with dia-
monds, being stoned to death. I prayed: If she must die,
let it only be some dream. But there were times, Mother,
while you slept, that I prayed, "Saints, let her die."
Not, I swear by you, that I wished you to die
but to save you as you were, young, in song in Kashmir,
and I, one festival, crowned Krishna by you, Kashmir
listening to my flute. You never let gods die.
Thus I swear, here and now, not to forgive the universe
that would let me get used to a universe

without you. She, she alone, was the universe
as she earned, like a galaxy, her right not to die,
defying the Merciful of the Universe,
Master of Disease, "in the circle of her traverse"
of drug-bound time. And where was the god of elephants,
plump with Fate, when tusk to tusk, the universe,
dyed green, became ivory? Then let the universe,
like Paradise, be considered a tomb. Mother,
they asked me, *So how's the writing?* I answered *My mother
is my poem.* What did they expect? For no verse
sufficed except the promise, fading, of Kashmir
and the cries that reached you from the cliffs of Kashmir

(across fifteen centuries) in the hospital. *Kashmir,
she's dying!* How her breathing drowns out the universe
as she sleeps in Amherst. Windows open on Kashmir:
There, the fragile wood-shrines—so far away—of Kashmir!
O Destroyer, let her return there, if just to die.
Save the right she gave its earth to cover her, Kashmir
has no rights. When the windows close on Kashmir,
I see the blizzard-fall of ghost-elephants.
I hold back—she couldn't bear it—one elephant's
story: his return (in a country far from Kashmir)
to the jungle where each year, on the day his mother
died, he touches with his trunk the bones of his mother.

"As you sit here by me, you're just like my mother,"
she tells me. I imagine her: a bride in Kashmir,
she's watching, at the Regal, her first film with Father.
If only I could gather you in my arms, Mother,
I'd save you—now my daughter—from God. The universe
opens its ledger. I write: How helpless was God's mother!
Each page is turned to enter grief's accounts. Mother,
I see a hand. *Tell me it's not God's.* Let it die.

I see it. It's filling with diamonds. Please let it die.
Are you somewhere alive, somewhere alive, Mother?
Do you hear what I once held back: in one elephant's
cry, by his mother's bones, the cries of those elephants

that stunned the abyss? Ivory blots out the elephants.
I enter this: *The Belovéd leaves one behind to die.*
For compared to my grief for you, what are those of Kashmir,
and what (I close the ledger) are the griefs of the universe
when I remember you—beyond all accounting—O my mother?

19

I

From Amherst to Kashmir

1. Karbala: A History of the "House of Sorrow"

*In a distant age and climate, the tragic scene
of the death of Husayn will awaken the sympathy
of the coldest reader.*

—EDWARD GIBBON

Jesus and his disciples, passing through the plain of Karbala, saw "a herd of gazelles, crowding together and weeping." Astonished, the disciples looked at their Lord. He spoke: "At this site the grandson of Prophet Muhammad (Peace be upon him) will one day be killed." And Jesus wept. *Oh, that my head were waters, and mine eyes a fountain of tears, that I might weep day and night for the slain . . .* And Jesus wept. And as if the news has just reached them—fourteen hundred years after the Battle of Karbala (near ancient Babylon, not far from the Euphrates) in the year A.H. 61/A.D. 680—mourners weep for "the prince among martyrs," Hussain, grandson of the Prophet and son of Ali ("Father of Clay") and Fatima (the Prophet's only surviving child). Memorializing Hussain on the tenth of Muharram (*Ashura*) is *the* rite of Shi'a Islam—so central that at funerals those events are woven into elegies, every death framed by that "Calvary." For just "as Jesus went to Jerusalem to die on the cross," Hussain "went to Karbala to accept the passion that had been meant for him from the beginning of time."

.

From the beginning of time? When Ishmael was saved, did the
ram suffice, even though Gabriel had brought it from Paradise,
from the very presence of God? Because both father as the slayer
and son as the victim had submitted to His will, God called out,
"Abraham, you have fulfilled the vision." And He ransomed
Ishmael with a "great redeeming sacrifice"—completed only
centuries later on the battlefield that became the altar. Abraham
foreknew all and wept bitterly. God spoke: "Abraham, through
your grief for Hussain, I have ransomed your grief for your son as
though you had slain him with your own hand."

·

At the call of the people of Kufa (their hearts were with him, their
swords with his enemies), Hussain, with his family and
supporters, set out from Mecca, "along the pilgrim route across
the desert of central Arabia," to challenge the tyranny of the
Caliph Yazid. In Karbala their caravan (2 Muharram 61/2 October
680) was intercepted by Yazid's troops under Obeidullah. Till the
tenth of Muharram, they withstood the siege, choosing death, not
surrender. Prevented from reaching the Euphrates, for three days
before the massacre they were without water. Anguished by the
children's cries, Abbas, Hussain's half brother, led a daring sortie
to fill a few waterskins but he perished.

·

On 9 Muharram, as if putting on his own shroud, Hussain spoke:
"Tomorrow our end will come. I ask you to go away to safety. I free
you, I do not hold you back. Night will give you a cover; use it as
a steed." He had the lights turned out. Fewer than one hundred
remained—among them the women, the children, the old.

·

And the borrowed night ends. They line up before the army. The rear of the tents is protected by wood and reeds set on fire. The first arrows come, in a shower. Hussain's nephew Qasim is struck and dies in his uncle's arms. Every man is killed. The women look on in terror. Alone, Hussain returns to the tents to console the children and women, among them his sister Zainab, and bids them farewell. At sunset, the soldiers turn to pillage. The bodies are decapitated, stripped of all covering. Hussain's severed head is brought to Obeidullah. He carelessly turns it over with his staff. "Gently," one officer protests. "By Allah! I have seen those lips kissed by the blessed mouth of Muhammad."

.

The morning of 12 Muharram saw seventy-two heads raised on lances, each held by a soldier, followed by the women on camels. One of Hussain's sons, the only male survivor, had lain sick during battle. The "adornment of God's servants," he was saved when Zainab threw herself over him. At the sight of the decapitated bodies, the women's lamentations rose: "O Muhammad! The angels of Heaven send blessings upon you, but this is your Hussain, so humiliated and disgraced, covered with blood and cut into pieces, and your daughters are made captives, your butchered family is left for the East Wind to cover with dust!" The head of Hussain was put on display in Kufa before it was sent to Yazid. Held in a dungeon, the captives before long were taken to Damascus.

.

Mourners beg for water—the martyrs' thirst. They wound their heads, and "the green grassy field" where their processions end "becomes bloodied and looks like a field of poppies." *And my brother knows he will die. He has himself put on his shroud.* A deluge of weeping follows. So I remember, since childhood. One *majlis*

Majlis: A gathering of people, specifically to mourn Karbala.

stays—Summer 1992—when for two years Death had turned every day in Kashmir into some family's Karbala. We celebrated *Ashura* with relatives, in the afternoon—because of night curfew. That evening, at home, my mother was suddenly in tears. I was puzzled, then very moved: Since she was a girl she had felt Zainab's grief as her own.

.

At my mother's funeral a mourner sang one of her favorite Kashmiri elegies, given to Zainab, in which her exile is nearly unbearable. Those words now are my mother's, for she too was tired, fighting death, from hospital to hospital, from city to city.

26

2. Zainab's Lament in Damascus

Over Hussain's mansion what night has fallen?

Look at me, O people of Shaam, the Prophet's
only daughter's daughter, his only child's child.

Over my brother's
bleeding mansion dawn rose—at such forever
cost?

   So weep now, you who of passion never
made a holocaust, for I saw his children
slain in the desert,
crying for water.

       Hear me. Remember Hussain,
what he gave in Karbala, he the severed
heart, the very heart of Muhammad, left there
bleeding, unburied.

Deaf Damascus, here in your Caliph's dungeons
where they mock the blood of your Prophet, I'm an
orphan, Hussain's sister, a tyrant's prisoner.

Father of Clay, he
cried, *forgive me. Syria triumphs, orphans
all your children. Farewell.*

Shaam: Arabic word for Syria.

And then he wore his
shroud of words and left us alone forever.

Paradise, hear me—
On my brother's body what night has fallen?

Let the rooms of Heaven be deafened, Angels,
with my unheard cry in the Caliph's palace:

Syria hear me

Over Hussain's mansion what night has fallen

I alone am left to tell my brother's story

On my brother's body what dawn has risen

Weep for my brother
World, weep for Hussain

3. Summers of Translation

Desolation's desert. I'm here with shadows
of your voice . . .
　　　　—FAIZ AHMED FAIZ, "Memory"

"Memory"—two years after your death they tell me—has
no translation. We knew it in a loved version,
the words languidly climbed by a singer of Faiz,

and, of course, we knew it well in the desolation
mastered by singers on Radio Pakistan
slowly-slowly . . . with shadows.
　　　　　　　　But it's a *bhajan*

from a black and white film, sung to a dark icon,
that I recall—the story, from every angle, bleak
(Dark blue god don't cast me into oblivion,

in the temples, all your worshippers are asleep):
As you told it, the child-bride would die, and the rain,
you remembered as a girl, would come each dawn to keep

her from what you longed for her. With thunder, a train—
from Pakistan?—would crash and bring down the refrain,

bhajan: Hindu devotional song.

and your tears. The train's whistle, years later, would rend
the heart.
    As I begin "Memory" all by myself
(I'll hold on to your sleeve, blue god, till the end),

so many summers, so many monsoons, dimmed on Time's shelf,
return, framed by the voice you gave to each story,
as when—in the last summer of peace—the heart itself

was the focus: You read all of Faiz aloud to me:
We chose poems that would translate best. So strange:
Why did we not linger just a bit on "Memory?"

It was '89, the stones were not far, signs of change
everywhere (Kashmir would soon be in literal
flames). Well, our dawns were so perfectly set to arrange

our evenings in color that liberty with each ghazal
was my only way of being loyal to any original . . .

I shelve "Memory" to hear Begum Akhtar enclose—
in Raga *Jogia*—the wound-cry of the gazelle:
"Not all, no, only a few return as the rose

or the tulip." That ghazal held under her spell.
But when you welcomed me in later summers to Kashmir,
every headline read:
            PARADISE ON EARTH BECOMES HELL.

The night was broken in two by the Call to Prayer
which found nothing to steal but my utter disbelief.
In every home, although Muharram was not yet here,

Zainab wailed. Only Karbala could frame our grief:
The wail rose: *How could such a night fall on Hussain?*
Mother, you remembered perfectly that *God is a thief*

when memory is a black and white film again
(*Dark Krishna,*
        don't let your Radha die in the rain):

Begum Akhtar: One of India's great singers, and the greatest ghazal singer of
all time.
Jogia: Among the more austere ragas.
Radha: Consort of Krishna.

You wait, at the end of Memory, with what befell
Zainab—
       from Karbala to Kufa to Damascus.
You are wearing black. The cry of the gazelle

fills the night. It is Zainab's cry. You cry it for us
so purely that even in memory it lets memory cease.
For your voice could make any story so various,

so new, that even terrible pain would decrease
into wonder. But for me, I who of passion
always make a holocaust, will there be a summer of peace?

A mother dies. There's a son's execution.
On Memory's mantle—where summers may truly shine—
all, as never before, is nothing but translation.

It is Muharram again.
                   Of God there is no sign.
Mother,
       you are "the breath drawn after every line."

4. Above the Cities

> God is the Light of the heavens and the earth—
> the likeness of His light is as a niche wherein
> is a lamp . . .
>
> —THE KORAN
> Surah 24:35

Boston-Frankfurt-Delhi. Lufthansa airborne,
coffin-holding coffin. Now home to Kashmir.
Was it prophesied what we, broken, gather?
She is with us and

we—without her? Where is the lamp that's "kindled
from a Bléssed Tree," that one olive which is
"neither of the East nor the West whose oil would
well-nigh keep shining

though untouched by fire"? For

> Doomsday but barely had taken its first breath
> when I remembered again the hour you left,

          Doomsday's very
first breath—which was but your departure—that I
learn by heart again and again. I'm piling
Doomsday on Doomsday

over oceans, continents, deserts, cities.
Airport after airport, the plane is darkness

plunged into the sunrise,

For I had also seen the moth rush to the candle—
then nothing but the wrenched flame gasping in knots.

So nothing then but
Karbala's slaughter

through my mother's eyes at the *majlis,* mourning
Zainab in the Damascene court, for she must
stand before the Caliph alone, her eyes my
mother's, my mother's

hers across these centuries, each year black-robed
in that 1992 Kashmir summer—
evening curfew minutes away: The sun died.
We had with Zainab's

words returned home:

Hussain, I'm in exile from exile, lost from
city to city.

Outside, the guns were punctual
stars. The night was Muharram's orphan-vigil,
she in sudden tears. "Mummy, what's the matter?"
"Nothing, it's Zainab's

grief, that's all." Her eyes are two candles darkened
with laments found lost on our lips,

Over Hussain's mansion what night is falling?

two candles

lit above the cities she'll never visit,
names that were spellbound

on her lips, their magic unbearable now—
Naples, Athens, Isfahan, Kashgar. Hush. For
over Hussain's mansion the night that's dropped is
leading the heart in

one jade line unbroken to Doomsday: *She is
gone!*—the nurse's words. And again the flat line
(*She is gone!*), for in the ICU green, the
monitor's pulse was

but the heart unable to empty itself.

    O bleeding mansion, what night has fallen?

She is gone! Now out of the cabin's blue dark,
blinding lights accompany *We'll be landing
shortly at Delhi*

Airport—city of my birth! Our descent is
just her voice (I'd crushed the dawn tablets into
spoons of water): *You must now write my story,
Bhaiya, my story*

only. On the shelf you're deluged with night-veiled
light, your face in that niche where memory, Mother,
darkens with the Light of the heavens.

    Zainab weeps for Hussain in Karbala's night.

Bhaiya: The author's pet name.

Still it's

easy to write your

story—you are even in lines in which you
can't be found. It's easy to write your story.
For whatever city I fly to, even
that of my birth, you

aren't there to welcome me. And any city
I am leaving—even if one you've never
seen—my parting words are for you alone. For
where there is farewell,

you are there. And where there's a son, in any
language saying *Adieu* to his mother, she is
you and that son (*There by the gate*) is me, that
son is me. Always.

5. *Memory*

from Faiz Ahmed Faiz

Desolation's desert. I'm here with shadows
of your voice, your lips as mirage, now trembling.
Grass and dust of distance have let this desert
bloom with your roses.

Near me breathes the air that's your kiss. It smoulders,
slowly-slowly, musk of itself. And farther,
drop by drop, beyond the horizon, shines the
dew of your lit face.

Memory's placed its hand so on Time's face, touched it
so caressingly that although it's still our
parting's morning, it's as if night's come, bringing
you to my bare arms.

6. New Delhi Airport

Whom the flame itself has gone searching for, that
moth—just imagine!
            —BOMBAY FILM SONG

Haze of April heat. We are on the tarmac.
Soon a journey's end will begin—and soon end.
How she longed for home, to return alive, go
home to light candles . . .

All the flames have severed themselves from candles,
darkened Kashmir's shrines to go find their lost one,
burning God the Moth in stray blasphemy. His
Wings have caught fire,

lit up broken idols in temples, on whom
Scripture breaks, breaks down to confess His violence:
what their breaking's cost the forsaken nation
that now awaits her

at the wind- and water-stretched end of Earth—to
which, veiled, she's being brought back from Goodbye's other
sky, the God-stretched end of the blue, returning
as the Belovéd,

final lonely rival to God. The flames, like
moths, look just for her. Will they, searching Kashmir,
be extinguished, longing for her and prophets?
All of a sudden

through the haze the crated shrine's taken past us.
When it's gone, I know she was trying to tell me—
what? For veiled, her voice is the veil itself. O
Father of Clay, your

daughter Zainab wanders in thirst. The Prophet's
blood is streams on Karbala's sands. What truth's here?
Hussain's dead and she's caught in exile, lost from
city to city.

Pilgrims brought back clay from that site of slaughter—
Karbala was chosen for Kashmir's seasons,
mixed into the graveyard's cold beds of roses.
We are such pilgrims

too, returning thus with her shrine. It enters
first the hold's, then memory's desolation.
Soon we climb the ramp, and the sky is empty
once we are airborne.

7. *Film* Bhajan *Found on a 78 RPM*

Dark god shine on me you're all I have left
nothing else blue god you are all I have
I won't let go I'll cling on to your robe

I am yours your Radha my bangles break
I break my bangles my heart is glass come back
blue god there's nothing you are all I have

let there be no legend of a lost one
who breaks her bangles who lets herself die
who says you hid yourself to break my heart

your eyes are my refuge hide me from the world
dark god Dark Krishna you are all I have
do not hide yourself merely to break my heart

all day I'm restless all night I can't sleep
the morning star sinks it drowns in my eyes
the night is heavy its dark is iron

take my hand place your hands in mine in yours
I'm yours dark god do not abandon me
all night I won't sleep even for a while

in the temples all the worshippers sleep
your flute strikes the stars its legends echo
and the soul in its trance crosses the sky

my heart keeps breaking does not stop breaking
it says dark god I will never leave you
the heart is awake it keeps on breaking

all night I'm awake I'll keep you awake
take this vow that I am yours I am yours
dark god you are all I have all I have

all night I'm awake I'll keep you awake
in your temples all the worshippers sleep
only swear I am yours that I am yours

only take this vow I am yours dark god
dark god you are all you are all I have
swear only swear I am yours I am yours

8. Srinagar Airport

There is no god but God.
    —THE KORAN

Only clouds. The rain has just stopped. And as her
shrine is onto Srinagar's tarmac lowered,
listen: Even they are here speechless, weeping,
those who of passion

never made a holocaust. One by one, they
hold me in their arms: *How could this have happened,
Bhaiya, how could it?* To the waiting van she's
brought on their shoulders.

Who are all these strangers for whom she rivals
God today? They stare. And we speed through streets that
follow *Farewell Farewell* and then at each turn
go into hiding—

for each turn's a world that recalls her, every
turn her world unable to say Goodbye, though
she, from every corner, is waving with such
pity we melt, melt

past the world she loved, past each corner she is
waving from, just waving herself goodbye. Who
doesn't owe her tears when we reach home and her
house—it is *her* house—

echoes with her keys? The doors open—she is
everywhere. Yes, here it must start, the FAREWELL,
from this very room, from its quiet center.
Outside, a man says,

"Soon it will be dark. We must reach the graveyard."
From the garden, echo to echo, voices
rise. "We must . . ." The afternoon darkens. She is
farther than any

god today and nearer than any god. And
God? He's farther, farther from us, forever
far. We lift the shrine. The women break into
There is no god but

9. God

"In the Name of the Merciful" let night begin.
I must light lamps without her—at every shrine?
God then is only the final assassin.

The prayers end. Emptiness waits to take her in.
With laments found lost on my lips, I resign
myself to His every Name. Let night begin

without any light, for as they carry the coffin
from the mosque to the earth, no stars shine
to reveal Him as only the final assassin.

The mourners, at the dug earth's every margin,
fill emptiness with their hands. Their eyes meet mine
when with no Name of His I let my night begin.

In the dark the marble of each tomb grows skin.
I tear it off. I make a holocaust. I underline
God is the only, the only assassin

as flames put themselves out, at once, on her shrine
(they have arrived like moths from temples and mosques).
In no one's name but hers I let night begin.

10. Ghalib's Ghazal

Not all, only a few—
    disguised as tulips, as roses—
        return from ashes.
What possibilities
    has the earth forever
        covered, what faces?

Time ago I too could recall
    those moon-lit nights,
        wine on the Saqi's roof—
But Time's shelved them now
    in its niche, in
        Memory's dim places.

Let me weep, let this blood
    flow from my eyes.
        She is leaving.
These tears, I'll say, have
    lit my eyes, two candles
        for love's darkest spaces.

What isn't his?
    He is Sleep, is Peace, is Night,
        mere mortal become god

Ghalib: He is to Urdu what Shakespeare is to English, Dante to Italian, and
Pushkin to Russian.
Saqi: One who pours wine.

when your hair lies scattered,
    shining, on his shoulder,
        he now one whom nothing effaces.

Wine, a giver of life! Hold the glass.
    The palm's lines, as one, will
        rush to life—
Here's my hand, its
    life-line beating, here
        Look! the glass it raises.

Man is numbed to pain
    when he's sorrow-beaten.
        Sorrows, piled up, ease pain.
Grief crushed me so
    again and again it became
        the pain that pain erases.

World, take note, should Ghalib
    keep weeping, you'll see
        only a wilderness
where you built
    your terraced cities,
        your marble palaces.

11. The Fourth Day

Doomsday had but—but barely had—breathed its first
when I again remembered you as you were leaving.
                                                —GHALIB

The dead—so quickly—become the poor at night.

And the poor? They are the dead so soon by night . . .

But whom the news has reached in the Valley of Death

(The Belovéd is gone The Belovéd is gone)

they are not the dead, they are the poor at dawn,

they who have come from shrines after breaking their heads on
     the threshold-stones of God.

                         . . .

When you left flames deserted their wicks in the shrines.

Now they arrive with the poor to light up the few who have
     returned from ashes, disguised as roses.

What possibilities the earth has forever covered, what faces?

The Fourth Day: Among Muslims, it marks the end of the first active period
of mourning.

They have arrived with wings, as burning moths, to put
    themselves out on your grave.

From behind headstones they keep coming with the dead—who
    are not the dead—

just the poor, wrapped in blankets, risen at dawn, walking like
    the dead by the wrecked river . . .

From behind headstones they keep coming toward us, silent on
    a carpet by your grave.

They are not the dead. We are the poor at dawn.

When the flames are wrenched, gasping in knots, they are not
    the dead. We are the poor at dawn.

And when the flames die, they leave what is left of their hands.

In fingerprints they leave all their prayers on your grave.

· · ·

Four days: And eternities have so quickly slowed down.

Only a few—disguised as roses—return from ashes.

They are the poor, not the dead at dawn, who have come to
    weep with all their passion:

Doomsday barely begins when it repeats its beginning

(For what is Doomsday but the Belovéd's departure?)

and I again remember you leaving with the caravan of dawn.

Four days have passed. Eternities have slowed down:

See, see where Hussain's blood streams the sands.

They are not the dead, we are the poor at dawn.

I stood weeping in the desert and the sun rose.

And the sun fell on the roofs of the poor. And it fell on
    mansions in the mountains.

Again I see you leave with the caravan of dawn.

Doomsday begins. It keeps on beginning.

And the Belovéd leaves one behind to die.

                       . . .

The sun has barely risen. They await us in the mosque.

We leave you alone; we leave the earth to you.

In the courtyard they are gathered. There's only Karbala in their
    hearts.

And Abraham weeps. And God's angels weep.

And the sun still beats in the desert:

See, see where Hussain's blood streams the desert.

And God's angels weep. And Jesus weeps.

The Belovéd leaves one behind to die.

And with the wounded gazelle's wail in his heart (It is Zainab's cry, It is Zainab's cry), an old man begins:

"Over Hussain's mansion what night has fallen . . ."

12. By the Waters of the Sind

Is the sinking moon like a prisoner
    sentenced somewhere to Black Water,
perhaps left hanged on the horizon
of an Andaman island? But here,
    in Kashmir, by these waters,
its light will leave me—where?

My father is—in Persian—reciting
    Hafiz of Shiraz, that "Nothing
in this world is without terrible
barriers— / Except love, but only when
    it begins." And the host fills
everyone's glass again.

So what is separation's geography?
    Everything is just that mystery,
everything is this roar that deafens:
this stream has branched off from the Indus,
    in Little Tibet, just to
find itself where Porus

miles down (there it will join the Jhelum)
    lost to the Greeks. It will become,
in Pakistan, the Indus again.
Leaning against the Himalayas
    (the mountains here are never
in the distance), wine-glass

in hand, I see evening come on. It is
	two months since you left us. So this
is separation? Sharpened against
rocks, the stream, rapid-cutting the night,
	finds its steel a little stained
with the beginning light,

and the moon must rise now from behind
	that one pine-topped mountain to find
us without you. I stare at one guest
who is asking Father to fill them
	in on—what else?—the future,
burnishing that dark gem

of Kashmir with a history of saints, with
	prophecy, with kings, and with myth,
and I want them to change the subject
to these waters that must already
	be silver there where the moon
sees the Indus empty

itself into the Arabian Sea. What
	rustle of trees the wind forgot
reaches me through this roar as the moon,
risen completely, silvers the world
	so ruthlessly, shining on
me a terror so pearled

that *How dare the moon*—I want to cry out,
	Mother—*shine so hauntingly out
here when I've sentenced it to black waves
inside me? Why has it not perished?
	How dare it shine on an earth
from which you have vanished?*

II

Rooms Are Never Finished

Many of my favorite things are broken.
—MARIO BUATTA, interior designer
known as "The King of Chintz"

In here it's deliberately dark so one may sigh

in peace. Please come in. How long has it been?
Upstairs—climb slowly—the touch is more certain.
You've been, they say, everywhere. What city's left?
I've brought the world indoors. One wants certainty.
Not in art—well, you've hardly changed—but, why,

in life. But for small invisible hands, no wall
would be lacquered a rain forest's colors. Before,
these walls had just mirrors (I tried on—for size—
kismet's barest air). Remember? You were
led through all the spare rooms I was to die

in. But look how each room's been refurbished:
This screen in stitches silk-routes a river
down Asia, past laughing Buddhas, China
a lantern burning burning burning for
"God to aggrandise, God to glorify"

in (How one passes through such thick walls!).
Candles float past inked-in laborers
but for whose hands this story would be empty,
rooms where one plots only to die, nothing
Dear! but a bare flame for you to come by

in. *Don't touch that vase!* Long ago
its waist, abandoned by scrolling foliage,
was banded by hands, banded quick with omens:
a galloping flood, hooves iron by the river's edge.
O beating night, what could have reined the sky

in? Come to the window: panes plot the earth
apart. In the moon's crush, the cobalt stars
shed light—blue—on Russia: the republics porcelain,
the Urals mezzotint. Why are you weeping,
dear friend? Hush, rare guest. Once a passerby

in tears, his footsteps dying, was . . . well, I rushed
out and he was gone. Out there it's poison.
Out there one longs for all one's ever bought,
for shades that lighten a scene: When the last leaves
were birds spent wingless on trees, love, the cage to cry

in, was glass-stormed by the North. Now that God
is news, what's left but prayer, and . . . well, if you
love something, why argue? What we own betters
any tale of God's—no? That framed scroll downstairs
and here! this shell drowned men heard God's reply

in. Listen, my friend. But for quick hands, my walls
would be mirrors. A house? A work in progress,
always. But: Could love's season be more than this?
I'll wipe your tears. Turn to me. My world would be
mere mirrors cut to multiply, then multiply

in. But for small hands. Invisible. Quick . . .

(for Matthew Stadler)

56

Ghazal

What will suffice for a true-love knot? Even the rain?
But he has bought grief's lottery, bought even the rain.

"our glosses / wanting in this world" "Can you remember?"
Anyone! when we thought the lovers taught even the rain?

After we died—*That was it!*—God left us in the dark.
And as we forgot the dark, we forgot even the rain.

Drought was over. Where was I? Drinks were on the house.
For mixers, my love, you'd poured—what?—even the rain.

Of this pear-shaped orange's perfumed twist, I will say:
Extract vermouth from the bergamot, even the rain.

How did the Enemy love you—with earth? air? and fire?
He held just one thing back till he got even: the rain.

This is God's site for a new house of executions?
You swear by the Bible, Despot, even the rain?

After the bones—those flowers—this was found in the urn:
the lost river, ashes from the ghat, even the rain.

What was I to prophesy if not the end of the world?
A salt pillar for the lonely lot, even the rain.

How the air raged, desperate, streaming the earth with flames—
to help burn down my house, Fire sought even the rain.

He would raze the mountains, he would level the waves;
he would, to smooth his epic plot, even the rain.

New York belongs at daybreak to only me, just me—
to make this claim Memory's brought even the rain.

They've found the knife that killed you, but whose prints are
    these?
No one has such small hands, Shahid, not even the rain.

Barcelona Airport

Are you carrying anything that could
be dangerous for the other passengers?

O just my heart   first terrorist
(a flame dies by dawn   in every shade)

Crescent-lit   it fits the profile
on your screen

          Damascene-green
in blood's mansions   (candle that burned
till its flame died   in blue corridors)

it's relit each time   it tries to exit
this body for another's   in another century

(Andalusia was   but to be missed)

Last week I went   to the Pyrenees
and then came here   for the year's farewell
to your city

          In your custom of countdowns
as the gongs were struck   I gulped each grape
(the heart skipped   its beats wildly):

Ten . . . Seven   the Year whirled in
to castanets   to strings DRUMS Two

DRUMS ONE! DRUMS *Champagne!*

So what white   will the heart wear
till the soul is   its own blood-filled crystal
ruby refuge   for a fugitive angel?

His wings waxed silver   to track the Atlantic
he won't—like   any body—let

the soul go   So delete my emerald beats
(in each color all night   a candle burns)

Hit ENTER   the Mediterranean
this minute   is uncut sapphire

And your Catalan sky?   Behold how to hide
one must . . . like God   spend all one's blue

(for Rafiq Kathwari)

60

A Secular Comedy

1. Heaven

Heaven's lovesick Mediterranean blue
paper (parchment thickened to sky to hide His
loneliness) now peels to reveal what's left of
all that was Heaven.

I, Earth's ghost, am here where the windows, broken,
still reveal that He has learned nothing from His
errors, clouds in cobwebs on ceilings, shredded
wings in the corners.

"Vanished days, how," Gabriel says, "we miss them."
Drink, for even God shall not remain. Satan's
voice? His voice preserved here till now? And perfect?
Who'd dare sing after

such a bitter melody? God is voiceless,
missing passion. All of His hands lie broken.
This is death? This fire of separation?
This is survival?

Songs I know! What unfinished pain that leads to
ghosts has brought me here, what unfinished business?
Empty, only wilderness veined inside me,
I, with no shadow?

Even You don't give me a shadow: Your Light—
all the lights of Heaven—are dimmed tonight. Is
this the anniversary—Love's expulsion—
Night of the Fallen

Angels? Who will sing now? Was there just poison
or some grief in You when he fell through Chaos—
Your Abyss—for nights, and his mad wings, raging,
deafened the soundproof

halls of Heaven? What is apart from legend?
But He doesn't answer. He lets His Light go
out completely. And I am left without a
chance of a shadow.

2. Earth

Sudden god, his head's on my melting shoulder:
gap in nature: Oregon: evening taxi:
neon-slow from . . . downtown to . . . Jantzen Beach where
sleep will abandon

night in rose-lit Doubletree's quiet lobby,
silence ripe for worship, the hour that's taken:
Over me he's pulling down Heaven. Will he
after my body

hear hearts breaking breaking in rooms he passes?
Every door awaits a returning lover,
corridors caught gleaming with wounds, the story
(Violence's) no one

tells going on and on. In a time like this one
stars are shredded. Who will decipher grief then?
Grief's the question asked as the given answer:
Grief is the answer,

midnight shot with pearls: like his gaze that rushes
toward me, the rapids of separation
whirling loud, my face held below the water-
fall of his time. He's

leaving? No, he's settling on me his gaze now,
entering my sleep. What remains of night he
owns, and he's its message to me, awake, his
hair on my shoulder.

3. Hell

Hell, then! Pandemonium's walls have diamonds.
We who lost our lovers on earth are welcome;
all are welcome, mirrored among the angels
lonely with pity.

Pity? Yes, for Heaven (To us what music,
we *who trade in love*) and for love's first story:
God and Satan—*Iblis*, first monotheist,
jealously guarding

God as only he could have known Him. "God's so
lonely . . . else would He," asks one fallen angel,
emphasizing *lonely*, "else would He, *would* He
punish man so? For

none of you can understand Him." Sorry,
now for God, and full of such longing myself
while on Earth he's missed in his ruined temples,
what can I do but

stare at sky-sized posters of God in mirrors?
Archived here, these stolen reflections, kisses
pressed on guarded tablets of Heaven's chipped Word,
numbered and signed by

God—and *him*? "Please tell us," the angels beg him.
Kiss and tell? Will that suit this devil-lover?

64

Framed in every mirror, now really smiling,
bevelled sapphire,

God to me is closer, he shrugs his shoulders,
than the jugular is to man, so even
now, bereft of love, I must guard God's secrets.
Call it perverse or—

"—What?" the angels, taking their wings off lightly,
say. *It's simpler,*" he interrupts, "*it's that. . . . Well,*
come and try"—he's pouring some wine—"*this vintage*
aged here in cellars,

Heaven's ruby. Under my wings I hid some
bottles just before I was pushed through exits,
breaking panes. What lovely reminder, this
wine, of that passion—

Heaven's nights, His blood, then His flesh, my open
wings that tightly closed to again be opened . . .
Stop. I must. This hour, my Belovéd Tyrant
surely is weeping."

The Nature of Temporal Order

from Alexander Pushkin (1799–1837)

Rites of iron—hour of the Crucifixion:
Magdalene is mute in the Tree's forgiving
shade, and in the sun, on the other side, the
Virgin. In epic

griefs, both Marys witness their one God nailed to
Life, His slow torment. And the Celebration's
carried out: They vanish, both women, unseen;
quick, in their place, two

sentries, ruthless, stand at the Cross's foot, as
if they guard the gates of the Viceroy's mansion.
Has the State then seized as its effects even
God and His sacred

blood—not just the nails and the wood? Please tell me
why you're here—to save Him from scavengers and
thieves? You broke His flesh, with your thorns you crowned Him.
Guards, let the reason

you've been sent be clearer. To sanctify Him,
He whose blood is wine, its astonished moment?
Or, more puzzling, faith has bewildered Order:
Could you be thinking

Adam's lost sons—tribe whom His Execution
saved—insult Him by their mere presence and must be

kept far? Or: It's simpler? You follow orders
so the Empire's

lords and ladies—tourists from Rome—may marvel
that the king of kings is their Caesar's captive,
hanged man they unhindered must watch as they on
Calvary stroll by.

Ghazal

Feel the patient's heart
Pounding—oh please, this once—

—JAMES MERRILL

I'll do what I must if I'm bold in real time.
A refugee, I'll be paroled in real time.

Cool evidence clawed off like shirts of hell-fire?
A former existence untold in real time . . .

The one you would choose: Were you led then by him?
What longing, O *Yaar*, is controlled in real time?

Each syllable sucked under waves of our earth—
The funeral love comes to hold in real time!

They left him alive so that he could be lonely—
The god of small things is not consoled in real time.

Please afterwards empty my pockets of keys—
It's hell in the city of gold in real time.

God's angels again are—for Satan!—forlorn.
Salvation was bought but sin sold in real time.

Yaar: Hindi word for friend.

And who is the terrorist, who the victim?
We'll know if the country is polled in real time.

"Behind a door marked DANGER" are being unwound
the prayers my friend had enscrolled in real time.

The throat of the rearview and sliding down it
the Street of Farewell's now unrolled in real time.

I heard the incessant dissolving of silk—
I felt my heart growing so old in real time.

Her heart must be ash where her body lies burned.
What hope lets your hands rake the cold in real time?

Now Friend, the Belovéd has stolen your words—
Read slowly: The plot will unfold in real time.

(for Daniel Hall)

On Hearing a Lover Not Seen for Twenty Years Has Attempted Suicide

I suspect it was over me.

Suicide Note*

I could not simplify myself.

* Found poem.

Ghazal

Where should we go after the last frontiers,
where should the birds fly after the last sky?

—MAHMOUD DARWISH

In Jerusalem a dead phone's dialed by exiles.
You learn your strange fate: You were exiled by exiles.

One opens the heart to list unborn galaxies.
Don't shut that folder when Earth is filed by exiles.

Before Night passes over the wheat of Egypt,
let stones be leavened, the bread torn wild by exiles.

Crucified Mansoor was alone with the Alone:
God's loneliness—Just His—compiled by exiles.

By the Hudson lies Kashmir, brought from Palestine—
It shawls the piano, Bach beguiled by exiles.

Tell me who's tonight the Physician of Sick Pearls?
Only you as you sit, Desert child, by exiles.

Match Majnoon (he kneels to pray on a wine-stained rug)
or prayer will be nothing, distempered mild by exiles.

Mansoor: Mansoor al-Hallaj, the great Muslim mystic martyr who was cruci-
fied in Baghdad for saying "I am the Truth."
Majnoon: Literally, "possessed" or "mad" because he sacrificed everything for love.

"Even things that are true can be proved." Even they?
Swear not by Art but, dear Oscar Wilde, by exiles.

Don't weep, we'll drown out the Call to Prayer, O Saqi—
I'll raise my glass before wine is defiled by exiles.

Was—after the last sky—this the fashion of fire:
Autumn's mist pressed to ashes styled by exiles?

If my enemy's alone and his arms are empty,
give him my heart silk-wrapped like a child by exiles.

Will you, Belovéd Stranger, ever witness Shahid—
two destinies at last reconciled by exiles?

The Purse-Seiner *Atlantis*

Black Pacific. "Shahid, come here, quick." A ship,
giant lantern held in its own light, the dark
left untouched, a phantom-ship with birds, no, moths,

giant moths that cannot die. Which world has sent
it? And which awaits its cargo's circling light,
staggered halo made of wings? The dark is still,

fixed around that moving lamp which keeps the light
so encased it pours its milk into itself,
sailing past with moths that cannot put themselves

out. What keeps this light from pouring out as light?
Beautiful in white, she says, "I'll just be back."
She goes inside. I fill my glass till I see

everything and nothing stare back at me, fill
me with longing, the longing to long, to be
flame, and moth, and ash. What light now startles me?

Neighbor's window. *Turn it off, God, turn it off.*
When they do, a minute later, I am—what?
Ash completely, yet not ash, I see I am

what is left of light, what light leaves me, what light
always leaves of me. "Oh, Shahid" (from inside
her voice is light), "could you light the candles, please?"

"Come back out, the ship is close." Moths, one by one,
dive into the light, dive deep to catch the light,
then return to keep the halo. Ship, what ghost

keeps you moving north? Your light is pouring flames
down your sides, yet all the sea keeps dark. What waits
for you beyond—seas and continents erased

from every map? The halo thickens. Yet what
keeps the sky untouched, so dark? She comes outside.
"Do you like the wine? I bought it years ago."

"It is the best ever." When I next look out
("Nothing lasts, of course"), the ship has disappeared.
The dark completes itself. What light now strikes us?

"Look, the phosphorus." It streaks the shore, it shines
green, bottle green, necklace darkened round the shore
where we now are walking by Time's stray wreckage

(broken planks, black glass) while the waves, again,
repeat each rumor the sea, out there, denies—
chilled necklaces, lost continents, casks of wine.

(for Elena Karina Byrne)

III

POEM BY MAHMOUD DARWISH

VERSION BY AGHA SHAHID ALI

(WITH AHMAD DALLAL)

Eleven Stars Over Andalusia

1. *On our last evening on this land*

On our last evening on this land we chop our days
from our young trees, count the ribs we'll take with us
and the ribs we'll leave behind . . . On the last evening
we bid nothing farewell, nor find the time to end . . .
Everything remains as it is, it is the place that changes our
    dreams
and its visitors. Suddenly we're incapable of irony,
this land will now host atoms of dust . . . Here, on our last
    evening,
we look closely at the mountains besieging the clouds: a
    conquest . . . and a counter-conquest,
and an old time handing this new time the keys to our doors.
So enter our houses, conquerors, and drink the wine
of our mellifluous *Mouwashah.* We are the night at midnight,
and no horseman will bring dawn from the sanctuary of the last
    Call to Prayer . . .
Our tea is green and hot; drink it. Our pistachios are fresh; eat
    them.
The beds are of green cedar, fall on them,
following this long siege, lie down on the feathers of our
    dreams.
The sheets are crisp, perfumes are ready by the door, and there
    are plenty of mirrors:
Enter them so we may exit completely. Soon we will search
in the margins of your history, in distant countries,

Mouwashah: The characteristic form of Andalusian poetry, recited and sung.
Still performed throughout the Arab world.

for what was once *our* history. And in the end we will ask
  ourselves:
Was Andalusia here or there? On the land . . . or in the poem?

2. How can I write above the clouds?

How can I write my people's testament above the clouds when
    they
abandon me as they do their coats at home, my people
who raze each fortress they build and pitch on its ruins
a tent, nostalgic for the beginning of palm trees? My people
    betray my people
in wars over salt. But Granada is made of gold,
of silken words woven with almonds, of silver tears
in the string of a lute. Granada is a law unto herself:
It befits her to be whatever she wants to be: nostalgia for
anything long past or which will pass. A swallow's wing brushes
a woman's breast, and she screams: "Granada is my body."
In the meadow someone loses a gazelle, and he screams,
    "Granada is my country."
And I come from there . . . So sing until from my ribs the
    goldfinches can build
a staircase to the nearer sky. Sing of the chivalry of those who
    ascend,
moon by moon, to their death in the Belovéd's alley. Sing the
    birds of the garden,
stone by stone. How I love you, you who have broken me,
string by string, on the road to her heated night. Sing how,
after you, the smell of coffee has no morning. Sing of my
    departure,
from the cooing of doves on your knees and from my soul
    nesting
in the mellifluous letters of your name. Granada is for singing, so
    sing!

3. There is a sky beyond the sky for me

There is a sky beyond the sky for my return, but
I am still burnishing the metal of this place, living in
an hour that foresees the unseen. I know that time
cannot twice be on my side, and I know that I will leave—
I'll emerge, with wings, from the banner I am, bird
that never alights on trees in the garden—
I will shed my skin and my language.
Some of my words of love will fall into
Lorca's poems; he'll live in my bedroom
and see what I have seen of the Bedouin moon. I'll emerge
from almond trees like cotton on sea foam. The stranger passed,
carrying seven hundred years of horses. The stranger passed
here to let the stranger pass there. In a while I'll emerge a stranger
from the wrinkles of my time, alien to Syria and to Andalusia.
This land is not my sky, yet this evening is mine.
The keys are mine, the minarets are mine, the lamps are mine,
and I am also mine. I am Adam of the two Edens, I who lost
    paradise twice.
So expel me slowly,
and kill me slowly,
under my olive tree,
along with Lorca . . .

4. I am one of the kings of the end

. . . And I am one of the kings of the end . . . I jump
off my horse in the last winter. I am the last gasp of an Arab.
I do not look for myrtle over the roofs of houses, nor do I
look around: No one should know me, no one should recognize
    me, no one who knew me
when I polished marble words to let my woman step
barefoot over dappled light. I do not look into the night, I mustn't
see a moon that once lit up all the secrets of Granada,
body by body. I do not look into the shadow, so as not to see
somebody carrying my name and running after me: Take your
    name away from me
and give me the silver of the white poplar. I do not look behind
    me, so I won't remember
I've passed over this land, there is no land in this land
since time broke around me, shard by shard.
I was not a lover believing that water is a mirror,
as I told my old friends, and no love can redeem me,
for I've accepted the "peace accord" and there is no longer a
    present left
to let me pass, tomorrow, close to yesterday. Castile will raise
its crown above God's minaret. I hear the rattling of keys
in the door of our golden history. Farewell to our history!
    Will I be
the one to close the last door of the sky, I, the last gasp of an
    Arab?

5. One day I will sit on the pavement

One day I will sit on the pavement . . . the pavement of the
    estranged.
I was no Narcissus; still I defend my image
in the mirrors. Haven't you been here once before, stranger?
Five hundred years have passed, but our breakup wasn't final,
and the messages between us never stopped. The wars
did not change the gardens of my Granada. One day I'll pass its
    moons
and brush my desire against a lemon tree . . . Embrace me and
    let me be reborn
from the scents of sun and river on your shoulders, from your
    feet
that scratch the evening until it weeps milk to accompany the
    poem's night . . .
I was not a passerby in the words of singers . . . I was the words
of the singers, the reconciliation of Athens and Persia, an East
    embracing a West
embarked on one essence. Embrace me that I may be born again
from Damascene swords hanging in shops. Nothing remains of
    me
but my old shield and my horse's gilded saddle. Nothing remains
    of me
but manuscripts of Averroes, *The Collar of the Dove*, and translations.
            · · ·
On the pavement, in the Square of the Daisy,
I was counting the doves: one, two, thirty . . . and the girls

The Collar of the Dove: A celebrated treatise on love by Ibn Hazm of Cordoba.

snatching the shadows of the young trees over the marble, leaving me
leaves yellow with age. Autumn passed me by, and I did not notice
the entire season had passed. Our history passed me on the pavement

. . .

and I did not notice.

6. Truth has two faces and the snow is black

Truth has two faces and the snow falls black on our city.
We can feel no despair beyond our despair,
and the end—firm in its step—marches to the wall,
marching on tiles that are wet with our tears.
Who will bring down our flags: we or they? And who
will recite the "peace accord," O king of dying?
Everything's prepared for us in advance; who will tear our names
from our identity: you or they? And who will instill in us
the speech of wanderings: "We were unable to break the siege;
let us then hand the keys to our paradise to the Minister of
    Peace, and be saved . . ."
Truth has two faces. To us the holy emblem was a sword
hanging over us. So what did you do to our fortress before this
    day?
You didn't fight, afraid of martyrdom. Your throne is your coffin.
Carry then the coffin to save the throne, O king of waiting,
this exodus will leave us only a handful of dust . . .
Who will bury our days after us: you . . . or they? And who
will raise their banners over our walls: you . . . or
a desperate knight? Who will hang their bells on our journey:
you . . . or a miserable guard? Everything is fixed for us:
why, then, this unending conclusion, O king of dying?

7. Who am I after the night of the estranged?

Who am I after the night of the estranged? I wake from my
    dream,
frightened of the obscure daylight on the marble of the house, of
the sun's darkness in the roses, of the water of my fountain;
frightened of milk on the lip of the fig, of my language;
frightened of wind that—frightened—combs a willow;
    frightened
of the clarity of petrified time, of a present no longer
a present; frightened, passing a world that is no longer
my world. Despair, be merciful. Death, be
a blessing on the stranger who sees the unseen more clearly than
a reality that is no longer real. I'll fall from a star
in the sky into a tent on the road to . . . where?
Where is the road to anything? I see the unseen more clearly
    than
a street that is no longer my street. Who am I after the night of
    the estranged?
Through others I once walked toward myself, and here I am,
losing that self, those others. My horse disappeared by the
    Atlantic,
and by the Mediterranean I bleed, stabbed with a spear.
Who am I after the night of the estranged? I cannot return to
my brothers under the palm tree of my old house, and I cannot
    descend to
the bottom of my abyss. You, the unseen! Love has no heart . . .
no heart in which I can dwell after the night of the estranged . . .

8. O water, be a string to my guitar

O water, be a string to my guitar. The conquerors arrived,
and the old conquerors left. It is difficult to remember my face
in the mirrors. Water, be my memory, let me see what I have lost.
Who am I after this exodus? I have a rock
with my name on it, on a hill from which I see what's long
    gone . . .
Seven hundred years escort me beyond the city wall . . .
In vain time turns to let me salvage my past from a moment
that gives birth to my exile . . . and others' . . .
To my guitar, O water, be a string. The conquerors arrived,
and the old conquerors left, heading southward, repairing their
    days
in the trashheap of change: I know who I was yesterday, but
    who will I be
in a tomorrow under Columbus's Atlantic banners? Be a string,
be a string to my guitar, O water! There is no *Misr* in Egypt,
no Fez in Fez, and Syria draws away. There is no falcon in
my people's banner, no river east of the palm groves besieged
by the Mongols' fast horses. In which Andalusia do I end? Here
or there? I will know I've perished and that here I've left
the best part of me: my past. Nothing remains but my guitar.
Then be to my guitar a string, O water. The old conquerors left,
the new conquerors arrived.

Misr: "urban life," but also "Egypt."
Fez: (Arabic *Fas*) also means "ax."

9. In the exodus I love you more

In the exodus I love you more. In a while
you will lock the city's gates. There is no heart for me in your
    hands, and no
road anywhere for my journey. In this demise I love you more.
After your breast, there is no milk for the pomegranate at our
    window.
Palm trees have become weightless,
the hills have become weightless, and streets in the dusk have
    become weightless;
the earth has become weightless as it bids farewell to its dust.
    Words have become weightless,
and stories have become weightless on the staircase of night.
    My heart alone is heavy,
so let it remain here, around your house,
barking, howling for a golden time.
It alone is my homeland. In the exodus I love you more,
I empty my soul of words: I love you more.
We depart. Butterflies lead our shadows. In exodus
we remember the lost buttons of our shirts, we forget
the crown of our days, we remember the apricot's sweat, we
    forget
the dance of horses on festival nights. In departure
we become only the birds' equals, merciful to our days, grateful
    for the least.
I am content to have the golden dagger that makes my
    murdered heart dance—

kill me then, slowly, so I may say: I love you more than
I had said before the exodus. I love you. Nothing hurts me,
neither air nor water . . . neither basil in your morning nor
iris in your evening, nothing hurts me after this departure.

10. I want from love only the beginning

I want from love only the beginning. Doves patch,
over the squares of my Granada, this day's shirt.
There is wine in our clay jars for the feast after us.
In the songs there are windows: enough for blossoms to explode.

I leave jasmine in the vase; I leave my young heart
in my mother's cupboard; I leave my dream, laughing, in water;
I leave the dawn in the honey of the figs; I leave my day and my
    yesterday
in the passage to the Square of the Orange where doves fly.

Did I really descend to your feet so speech could rise,
a white moon in the milk of your nights . . . pound the air
so I could see the Street of the Flute blue . . . pound the evening
so I could see how this marble between us suffers?

The windows are empty of the orchards of your shawl. In
    another time
I knew so much about you. I picked gardenias
from your ten fingers. In another time there were pearls for me
around your neck, and a name on a ring whose gem was
    darkness, shining.

I want from love only the beginning. Doves flew
in the last sky, they flew and flew in that sky.
There is still wine, after us, in the barrels and jars.
A little land will suffice for us to meet, a little land will be
    enough for peace.

11. Violins

Violins weep with gypsies going to Andalusia
Violins weep for Arabs leaving Andalusia

Violins weep for a time that does not return
Violins weep for a homeland that might return

Violins set fire to the woods of that deep deep darkness
Violins tear the horizon and smell my blood in the vein

Violins weep with gypsies going to Andalusia
Violins weep for Arabs leaving Andalusia

Violins are horses on a phantom string of moaning water
Violins are the ebb and flow of a field of wild lilacs

Violins are monsters touched by the nail of a woman now
    distant
Violins are an army, building and filling a tomb made of marble
    and *Nahawund*

Violins are the anarchy of hearts driven mad by the wind in a
    dancer's foot
Violins are flocks of birds fleeing a torn banner

Violins are complaints of silk creased in the lover's night
Violins are the distant sound of wine falling on a previous desire

Nahawund: One of the classical Arabic musical modes.

Violins follow me everywhere in vengeance
Violins seek me out to kill me wherever they find me

Violins weep for Arabs leaving Andalusia
Violins weep with gypsies going to Andalusia

IV

I Dream I Am at the Ghat of the Only World

A night of ghazals comes to an end. The singer
departs through her chosen mirror, her one diamond
cut on her countless necks. I, as ever, linger

till chandeliers dim to the blue of Samarkand
domes and I've again lost everyone. Which mirror
opened for JM's descent to the skeletoned

dark? Will I know the waiting boat? The burnt water?
By which mirror Eqbal, in his clear undertone,
still plots to end all human pain? When my mother

died, he had wept so far away in Pakistan . . .
In the growing dark, through my own mirror, steps lead me
to the boat. From which time do I know the oarsman?

Don't you know me? You were a mere boy. For no money
I—I was a young man then—I always rowed you across
the Jhelum, of which this river's the ebony

ghost. Every wave I left untouched became glass
to reflect you. I left you untouched, I left you
perfect.

SO IT'S ANOTHER CHRONICLE OF LOSS . . .

JM: James Merrill. He speaks in capitals in the manner of voices from the other
world in his epic *The Changing Light at Sandover.*
Eqbal: Eqbal Ahmad, celebrated political thinker and activist who died in 1999.

AND LOVE. "Whose voice was that, fine out of" CLEAR DARK
   BLUE?
One who forsook you by dying, the way you forsook
me, and so many, by not dying. I've waited through—

what haven't I waited through?—but he's left a book
for you (I rowed him not long ago). It's right there.
I promised him I would keep it safe for you. Look

for it under your seat cushion. I find it. In fear
it will disappear I clutch it. Like a lost will,
a card falls out, its lowercase inked in austere

black: "Before his untimely death, James Merrill
requested" . . . I stop, for his heartstopping absence,
then finish: "Before his untimely death, James Merrill

requested that a copy of A SCATTERING OF SALTS,
now his last book, be sent to you with his compliments."

                          · · ·

The oarsman (SLAVE OF THE PROPHET . . . *That* was his
   name) . . .
The clock bell chimes, as it always did, in the Convent's
tower. Will he take me to the islands through the same

waters I know? The school day ends. The children's
laughter fills the waves. "Gula, keeper of our decades"
(I glance, *a look askance,* through the table of contents),

Gula the boatman: Gula is an affectionate name for Ghulam Mohommed
(Slave of Mohommed).

"I know you now." *You've kept me waiting. In the shades*
of islands they await letters their living have sent,
they whom (restless by the shrines) nothing persuades

of their own death. But is she here, magnificent
still if this world's emptied of music? Will I find her?
With her I'd heard—on 78 rpm—*Peer Gynt* . . .

and Ghalib's grief in the voice of Begum Akhtar
(diamonded singer who, just moments ago, chose
her own mirror). What hadn't we heard together—

and said—by the river of which this is the ghost?
Upstream, after Zero Bridge . . . through a narrow canal
he rows. From somewhere it is "Ase's Death." We coast

along flood banks. Now the iron gates to the Dal.
The music stops. "Will the authorities allow
the gates to open?" *The times are tyrannical*

and death is punctual. But as in boyhood, somehow
Gula has threatened with Hell or bribed with Heaven
some sleeping guard. We row past PARADISE ENOW,

GULISTAN, FIRDAUSI, SHIRAZ, even
KHAYYAM. From each houseboat tourists from long ago
wave, longing for letters, frantic to tear open

Dal: Legendary lake, famous for its luxury houseboats and floating gardens.
PARADISE ENOW, etc.: Houseboats with names (except for PARADISE
ENOW) of Persian poets.

envelopes. But they are stilled, always a tableau
when we approach. Gula leaves by their feet, in silence,
the letters I have brought, then returns to row

us, faster faster—*We should not keep your loved ones
waiting*. When I look back, nothing at all is heard
though I can see them furious in oblivion's

shade, crumpling postcards. *To whom will I row some word
of them when their wails have not even begun to die?*
An island of burnt chinars appears, bulbuls blurred—

without song—in their branches. What one could prophesy
in their shade is now lost to elegies in a shrine.
Gula always had candles for tombs, to occupy

their shades when he brought me here—always by design—
for by his secret cash in the back, once afloat,
he showed me, right here, jasmine sticks for the Divine.

• • •

But the trees have vanished when I step off the boat.
Instead there is a house, the one in Amherst, the one
where my mother fought death, by heart able to quote—

to the last—from the Urdu of Ghalib, from the Persian
of Hafiz. I keep ringing the bell. Eqbal Ahmad
opens the door, embraces me, "Where's the oarsman?

You should have asked him in." "There's only news of blood
out there in Kashmir. Whom will he ferry while
I'm here with you? I can't tell. But before the flood—

chinar: giant plane tree.
bulbul: Persian songbird reminiscent of the nightingale.

it's raining hard—he must let the dead reconcile
themselves to their shores." I run from window to window—
the boat is still moored. "Shahid, when you smile,

it seems your mother has returned to life. We all know
how you—you all—miss her. You all kept her alive
all those months, how you all fought death with her, although

love doesn't help anyone finally survive.
But she knew you would keep her alive, that you were
completely in love with her. Now *Khuda Hafiz*. I've

nothing more to say, for even here a voyager,
I always move in my heart between sad countries.
But let it not end" IT WON'T "this grief for your mother.

She is on the shrine-island where the Kashmiris,
from martyred voices, salve their every dirge, sublime
till the end." "What will she do when I'm on my knees

in the shrine? And Gula, where to now?" *We have time
left for only one destination, so we must
bypass the magic I've told you of, island where I'm*

*always given a dream, sole letter one of the dead entrusts
to me to row safely to someone terribly missed,
someone among the living. Eqbal asked me just*

today if his dream . . . "Yes, it was the catalyst
whereby I lost all fear of death, hearing him aslant,
'I am in a beautiful place, but to exist

Khuda Hafiz: "God be with you" in Farsi.

101

here is so lonely.'" *Now he'll have peace, for he can't*
send any more dreams. "Tell him it's reached every shore,
that it lives in the world, on its own, resonant

with no change, that it is safe with us evermore,
that it is only with his dream that you could pave
your way through these waves to me. For in each wave your oar

hits I die, no longer untouched. In each I am slave,
Slave of the Prophet, to you. What else can be mine?
I do not forsake you. How long before the saint's grave?"

We are almost there. Here, take my candles, my jasmine.
Remember, our time will be brief here. We are hardly
here, waves have lost their ebony shine. Inside the shrine

Our time will be brief here
                I see desecration, God's tapestry
ripped, the faded chant of "There is no god but God
and Mohammed . . ." emptied of its eternity.

Only the wind—since when?—has lived here, in one awed
fright of boots, of soldiers. Now the cry of the gazelle—
it breaks the heart into the final episode.

Already it is night? Or light? Here one cannot tell.
She ties round my wrist (I'm on my knees) the saint's thread:
"May this always keep you safe from the flames of Hell."

                       • • •

With a night of ghazals, what else comes to an end?
If steps bring her back from the river, will Eqbal
also climb to the back of his glass with some legend

of freedom? We wait by his mirror in the hall.
On which unknown future—or past—does all depend?
Again the air awaits "Morning Mood" or a ghazal

to be what survives after sacrilege, to rend
the light—or dark—as chandeliers dim. I look out
the shrine's blood-stained panes to see curtains descend

on all sides of the boat. Still among the devout,
I cry, "Mother, will I lose you again, and in this,
the only world left? Won't the world, ashamed without

you, find its shrines bereft of any premise
of God?" She enters the boat. I run out in the rain.
"Will I wait here, alone, by this ebony abyss,

abandoned by you, alone?" WITH THE GREAT GOD PAIN
"Son, live long, I've died to wait for you all your life.
So you won't weep night and day for me, or the slain,

I will tighten this thread." "But this is the knife that"
NEVER FALLING KILLS?
                                    Weep, for this is farewell,
To be rowed forever is the last afterlife

I cry out by the shrine door "I am no infidel
but on my knees on shore the believer in the rain—"
This is farewell I have rowed you this is farewell

"—believer Mother still on his knees in the rain
who knows that you even veiled are the one who employs
her touch like a lamp to show me again and again

to myself." AND THE LOVER COLDER AND WISER destroys
all hope . . . He is Death . . . His is the moving finger . . .
The boat enters fog . . . which thickens to clear . . . for one
    voice:

WEEPING? YOU MUST NOT. I ask, "Which world will bring
    her
back, or will he who wears his heart on his sleeve eaves-
drop always, in his inmost depths, on a cruel harbinger?"

SHAHID, HUSH. THIS IS ME, JAMES. THE LOVED ONE
    ALWAYS LEAVES.

Notes

Lenox Hill

"War's annals will fade into night / Ere their story die" is a direct quotation from Thomas Hardy's poem, "In Time of 'The Breaking of Nations.' "

Karbala: A History of the "House of Sorrow"

Most of this information—and some of the phrasing—is from Will Durant, *The Age of Faith*; Sayyid Muhammad Husayn Tabatabatai, *Shi'a*; David Pinault, *The Shiites*; Heinz Halm, *Shi'a Islam: From Religion to Revolution*; and S. Husain M. Jafri, *Origins and Early Development of Shi'a Islam*. Except for a few details, the basic information is the same in all histories of Karbala.

To establish primacy for Ishmael (Father of the Arab nation), in Islam it is Ishmael—not Isaac—whom God asked Abraham to sacrifice.

By the Waters of the Sind

Black Water: The phrase came to be, and continues to be, synonymous with forced labor and life imprisonment. *Kalapani*, or black water, referred to the stretch of ocean between mainland India and colonial Britain's most notorious prison on the Andaman islands. To cross *kalapani* meant being condemned to permanent exile.

A Secular Comedy

One Sufi interpretation of the God/Satan myth portrays Satan (*Iblis*) as being in love with God, and thus the jealous lover when God asks him to bow to Adam. In his refusal to bow, he fulfills God's secret wish, for God is the Belovéd, and Satan the true monotheist. Satan says to God,

"When You created me, you told me to bow to no one but You. Thus, I'm truer to Your word than You are." Hell is the absence of the Belovéd. (Evidence is now being discovered that Milton was familiar with this Sufi interpretation.)

Eleven Stars Over Andalusia

In the fall of 1993, I was sent a very literal version of this poem (called simply "Eleven Stars" in the Arabic) and asked to "convert it into poetry." Ahmad Dallal—who was then teaching at Smith College—went over that version with me, comparing it line by line with the Arabic original. As he did so, I took many notes and, some weeks later when I felt stymied, I decided to re-read Lorca (something that occurred to me because of the poem's reference to him). It was while reading Lorca that I found a way to tackle the task.

The phrase "Eleven stars" comes directly from The Koran (Surah 12:4): "Joseph said to his father: 'Father, I dreamt of eleven stars and the sun and the moon; I saw them prostrate themselves before me.' 'My son,' he replied, say nothing of this dream to your brothers lest they plot evil against you.' "

About the Author

Agha Shahid Ali, a Kashmiri-American, was born in New Delhi and grew up in Kashmir. Currently on the poetry faculty of the M.F.A./Ph.D Program at the University of Utah as well as the poetry faculty of the low-residency M.F.A. Program for Writers at the Warren Wilson College, he has taught at Hamilton College and the University of Massachusetts-Amherst and held visiting appointments at Princeton, Binghamton, New York University, and elsewhere. Author of several collections of poetry, among them *The Half-Inch Himalayas*, *A Nostalgist's Map of America*, and, most recently, *The Country Without a Post Office*, he is also a translator (Faiz Ahmed Faiz, *The Rebel's Silhouette: Selected Poems*), scholar (*T. S. Eliot as Editor*), and editor (*Ravishing DisUnities: Real Ghazals in English*). He has won Guggenheim, Ingram-Merrill, and other fellowships.